CD INCLUDED

HAL•LEONARD
BIG BAND
PLAY-ALONG
VOLUME 3

ALTO SAX

Duke Ellington

ISBN: 978-1-4234-4976-8

HAL•LEONARD®
CORPORATION
7777 W. BLUEMOUND RD. P.O. BOX 13819 MILWAUKEE, WI 53213

Visit Hal Leonard Online at
www.halleonard.com

CARAVAN

**Words and Music by DUKE ELLINGTON,
IRVING MILLS and JUAN TIZOL**

Arranged by MICHAEL SWEENEY

Alto Sax

ALTO SAX

CHELSEA BRIDGE

By BILLY STRAYHORN
Arranged by MARK TAYLOR

Alto Sax

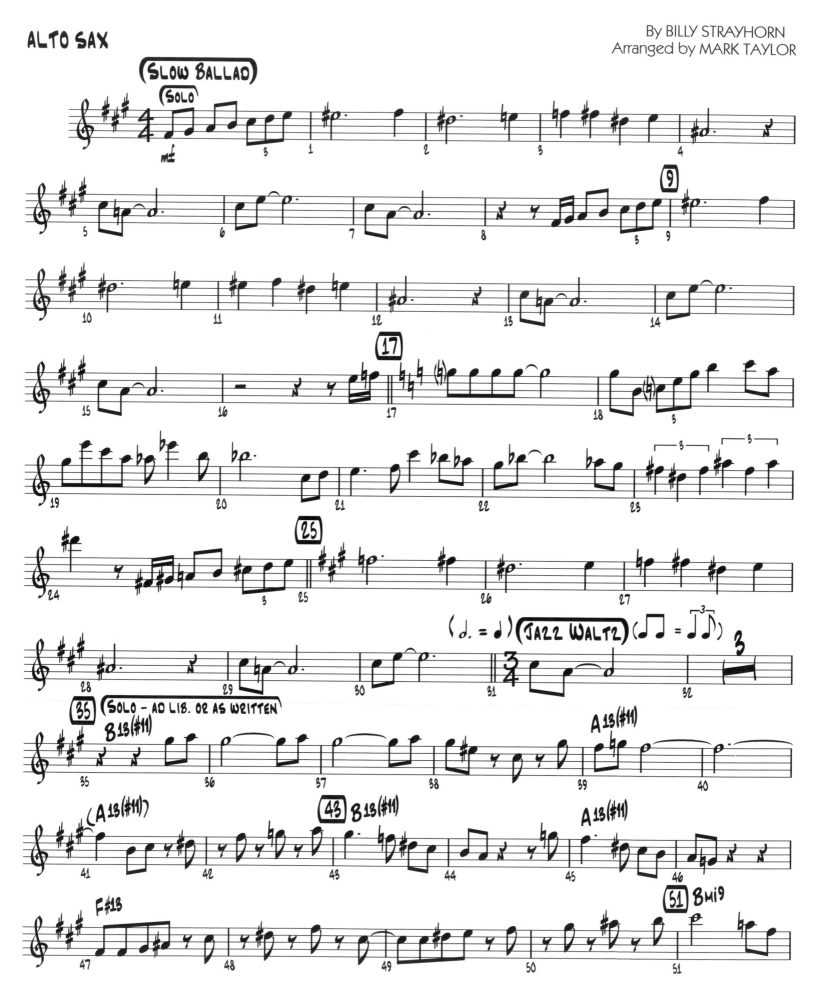

ALTO SAX

COTTON TAIL

Alto Sax

By DUKE ELLINGTON
Arranged by MARK TAYLOR

ALTO SAX

ALTO SAX

THIS PAGE HAS BEEN LEFT BLANK TO ACCOMMODATE PAGE TURNS.

Featured in SOPHISTICATED LADIES

I'M BEGINNING TO SEE THE LIGHT

Words and Music by DON GEORGE, JOHNNY HODGES,
DUKE ELLINGTON and HARRY JAMES

Arranged by MARK TAYLOR

Alto Sax

ALTO SAX

I'M JUST A LUCKY SO AND SO

Words by MACK DAVID
Music by DUKE ELLINGTON
Arranged by ROGER HOLMES

ALTO SAX

ALTO SAX

IN A MELLOW TONE

Alto Sax

By DUKE ELLINGTON
Arranged by MARK TAYLOR

ALTO SAX

IN A SENTIMENTAL MOOD

Alto Sax

By Duke Ellington
Arranged by MARK TAYLOR

MOOD INDIGO

Alto Sax

Words and Music by DUKE ELLINGTON,
IRVING MILLS and ALBANY BIGARD
Arranged by JOHN BERRY

ALTO SAX

D.S. AL CODA

⊕ CODA

SATIN DOLL

By DUKE ELLINGTON
Arranged by MARK TAYLOR

ALTO SAX

ALTO SAX

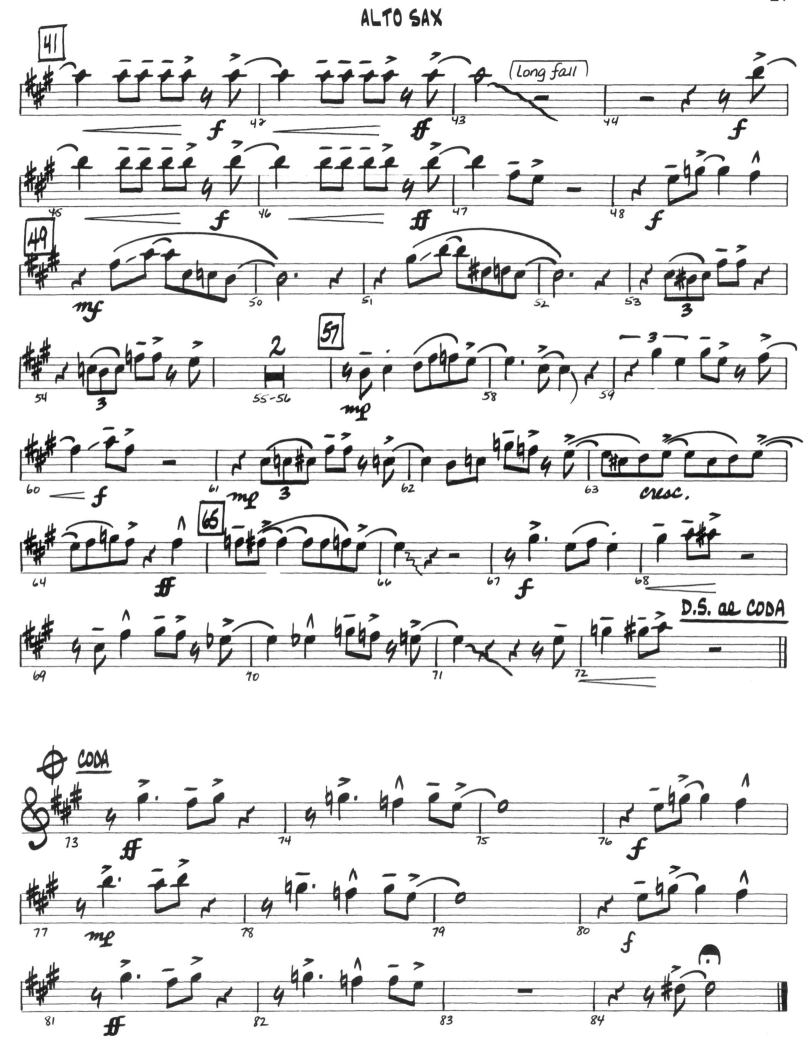

TAKE THE "A" TRAIN

Words and Music by
BILLY STRAYHORN
Arranged by DAVE BARDUHN

ALTO SAX

ALTO SAX